Yugoslavia
in color

Yugoslavia
in color

Photographs by F. A. H. BLOEMENDAL

Text by ANNE WARD

Charles Scribner's Sons
NEW YORK

Introduction

As a political entity, Yugoslavia has only existed since 1918. Before this it was a group of separate states which were occasionally independent republics or monarchies, but more often pushed and pulled about between Venetians, Turks, Austrians, Hungarians and various lesser tyrants, with an inextricably tangled footnote known to history books as the Macedonian Question thrown in on the southern side for good measure. Dalmatia, Croatia, Montenegro, Macedonia, Slovenia, Serbia, Bosnia and Hercegovina, with their shifting frontiers and innumerable sub-provinces, had little in common — not even a single language or script. The conspiracy to rob Yugoslavia of peace and unity seems even to extend to nature, for the raw materials of the area are so unevenly distributed as inevitably to raise a good deal of internal dissension. There are plenty of mineral deposits — gold and silver as well as copper, nickel and chromium — and no shortage of timber, oil and coal, but only in recent years has there been any constructive attempt to make use of these advantages.

The Yugoslavs have always preferred to think of themselves as an agricultural people, and until as late as the end of World War II 'peasant' was regarded as a proud appellation. The farming communities, however, were far from being uniformly fortunate in the resources at their disposal. The north-eastern plain is rich and fertile, and if ever a surplus was grown at all this was the area which produced it, but the mountain hinterland right down to the Adriatic is so harsh and inhospitable that the people's lives have been a perpetual struggle for survival. The inhabitants of this forbidding region necessarilly developed a certain fierce independence and stoic fortitude of character. They needed it, for even in the few coastal districts where the climate was mild enough for olive and mulberry trees, which provided the modest prosperity of a small oil and silk industry, the Venetian overlords of early Dalmatia, afraid for their own commercial supremacy, cut the trees down and restored the grim status quo for centuries.

In a land where city and country dwellers were always worlds apart, their frequently conflicting, if not actively hostile, interests could only add internal disruption to the devastation caused by invaders from abroad. The fact that it has ultimately proved possible to weld such disparate elements together into an effective state speaks volumes for the spirit of the people and the quality of their leaders.

The beginnings of the new Yugoslavia in 1918 were far from auspicious, for to the world at large the name meant only one thing: Sarajevo. This was the place where the heir to the Austrian throne was assassinated with his wife, thus precipitating all the horrors of World War I, which could hardly be a worse public image for the emergent nation. On the domestic front, too, never was an act of union carried out by a people with more disunited ideas, insofar as they had any clear plans at all about the constitution of their future state. When the National Council voted for the uniting of all the southern Slavs under the Karageorgevic dynasty there was only one dissenter; but he was the leader of the Peasant Party, and the peasants comprised four-fifths of the population, as the entire country boasted only three towns of more than ten thousand inhabitants (Belgrade, Zagreb and Subotica).

If this seems an unpromising start, the surprising thing is that the idea of nationalism ever entered Yugoslav heads at all, for their past history contained nothing but the faintest and most distant intimations of union. The notion arose only twice in earlier times, awakened on both occasions, oddly enough, by two of the greatest imperialist powers of all time —

the Romans and Napoleon, the first of whom established and the second of whom revived the province of Illyria, with its implications of brotherhood and a community of interests among the southern Slavs. Though Napoleon's Illyrian enterprise lasted less than a decade it did more to cement national feeling than all the troubled centuries of Balkan history, but after the fall of the French empire a hundred years of painful struggle were to elapse before union was finally achieved.

Practically the only thing the Yugoslavs had in common in 1918 was a fierce and unshakable determination to be one people, and at this stage they had given virtually no thought to finding a solution for the overwhelming problems which faced the mergent state, and which might well have daunted a more experienced legislature. The leaders of the Peasant Party seem to have laboured under the impression that the most constructive way they could represent their supporters (the vast majority of the electorate) was to retire into dignified isolation and refuse to acknowledge the existence of any action they did not approve, thus leaving their adversaries a completely clear field for the establishment of unopposed minority rule. The Constituent Assembly thereupon became a battlefield for monarchists versus republicans, centralists versus federalists, and for Catholics versus Orthodox versus Moslems, with the great agricultural majority, for all practical purposes, unrepresented because of their leaders' policy of non-cooperation.

Yugolslavia's first ten years were spent in coping slowly but steadily with the practical and material problems besetting the people. The rudiments of modern agricultural techniques were gradually introduced to farmers whose previous methods had been little short of mediaeval. The area under cultivation was extended and this, in combination with a lucky series of good harvests, in time produced a surplus which provided food for everyone and left over enough for export. The Yugoslavs, snugly entrenched in their agricultuaral economy, even managed to escape the financial crisis which brought such hardship to many of the more industrialized countries in 1929. A railway from Zagreb to Split was built, giving the inland mountain regions their first direct connection with the coast, and encouraging both trade and the tourist business.

Life at the political tóp, however, presented a less edifying spectacle. Statesmen formed alliances and coalitions, announced inviolable principles, and then back-tracked and changed partners with all the alacrity but none of the grace or predictability of a square-dance, leaving a trail of disillusioned and betrayed supporters at every turn. Regional differences seemed so impossible to reconcile that at one time there was even talk of breaking off Croatia and Slavonia and leaving them to fend for themselves as a separate state: a solution which would have solved nothing, for the Croats and Slavs were only too uncomfortably aware that in this event their immediate fate would be partition between Italy and Hungary, poised on their borders avidly awaiting the outcome. In the end all this political gerrymandering reached its inevitable conclusion in an ugly event which brought the whole problem to a head. A fanatically Radical deputy came to a meeting of Parliament armed with his own idea of the final solution and shot the two chief leaders of the Peasant Party. In the ensuing public outcry the constitution was temporarily suspended and the king took over personal control of the country in response to the demand for a single firm hand to replace the previous chaos of instability.

The nature of the new government was soon made abundantly clear. It was a harsh personal dictatorship aimed at the forcible suppression of terrorism and seditious activities, and at the ending of regional bickering by stamping out local differences and the enforcement of nationwide standards and practices. The Croats could no longer complain that the Serbs were being favoured at their expense, as both groups were being homogenized with sweeping impartiality. Inevitably, in the process of repressing sedition and provincialism, a number of perfectly harmless and innocent people were caught up in the machinery and suppressed along with the terrorists, while many civil liberties were curbed or cancelled. As to regional differences, the people prided themselves on their local characteristics and saw no reason why they should sink their identities in the new and unfamiliar corporate concept of "Yugoslavia" which, for the vast majority, held neither meaning nor tradition.

King Alexander's personal rule lasted only from 1929 to 1931, when he decided that it might be advisable to distribute the responsibility for his less popular measures by recalling Parliament. The newly summoned members met the situation by passing a whole series of apparently libertarian proclamations which, in practice, embodied so many limitations in the "small print" as to be virtually worthless. At this time most of the steps towards the unification of the different regions had a carefully concealed tendency to favour Serbian preferences as the norm to which the whole country was required to adhere. Cautious though the Serbianizing movement was, however, many non-Serbs saw through it and bitterly resented it. Political unrest within Yugoslavia was now being aggravated by an economic crisis. The years of good harvests came to an end, and it was Yugoslavia's ill fortune that they did so at the precise time when western Europe and America were in the grip of the worst effects of the great depression and could do little or nothing to help. The peasants helplessly watched their crops dwindling and their debts mounting, while shortage of winter fodder forced them to kill off the cattle which were the mainstay of their domestic food supplies and future prosperity.

Casting about for friends and allies in this desperate state of affairs, the king began to make overtures to the neighbouring states of Turkey, Romania, Greece and, more tentatively, Bulgaria, in an attempt to strengthen Balkan unity against the hostility or indifference of the longer-established nations. None of his new allies, however, was in a position to provide any financial backing for Yugoslavia, and the king realized that his best hope in this respect was France, which had always been sympathetically disposed. On October, 1934 the king landed at Marseilles on his way to discuss finances with the French government, and was almost immediatly murdered by an exiled Croatian separatist. Alexander had been obliged to make many highly unpopular moves, but the anger, shock and grief of his people on hearing of his death was a measure of their feeling for him. They recognized that, in the eyes of the outside world at least, he was a symbol of the Yugoslav unity and national stability which were at that time still more of a future dream than a present reality.

The boy king Peter II was represented by a three-man regency in which the leading role was played by Alexander's cousin, Prince Paul. Educated in Russia and at Oxford, Paul was regarded with considerable suspicion by many of the people. Initially, his main policy was to preseve things as they were until the nation was used to him and custom had bred acceptance. He therefore called in a ministry of politicians who were known to favour the 7 *status quo.* and the only changes he ordered were a few minor gestures of conciliation. However, when elections were held the following May, they conformed to a now familiar pattern; the electorate was issued with a mandate which amounted to: "You may vote for whomsoever you like so long as it is the official candidate". Even so, it was a close-run thing and the government's majority was so small as to make distinctly farcical showing, considering the unscrupulous silencing of the opposition's mouthpieces before and during the voting. The outrageous way in which these elections were conducted caused so much discontent that Prince Paul had to make hurried concessions. He sent for several members of the opposition and a new, cautiously liberal ministry was formed.

Everyone now seemed to be agreed that the Yugoslav states must all have a degree of federal independence, but this, of course, instantly opened the door to a clamorous outburst of quarrels over provincial boundaries. These disagreements, oddly enough, were partially reconciled by the agricultural population's common dislike of the government's increasing cordiality towards Nazi Germany. Pro-German links first began to solidify after World War I, when Germany's reparations were partially paid in the form of the technical and industrial machinery Yugoslavia needed so badly, but was not yet equipped to produce at home. From this time onwards, commercial exchanges grew more frequent and lucrative for both sides, the Germans providing the materials of heavy industry in return for Yugoslav agricultural produce. By 1937 this friendly attitude had become so strongly entrenched in official circles that Belgrade watched the Nazi annexation of Austria with complacence, if not active approval. The government might look benignly on Nazi expansion, but the Serbs and Croats, for once in their history, drew temporarily closer together in mutual alarm at the rapid growth of the anti-democratic colossus which was now so near to their own lands.

Public distrust became too apparent to be ignored after the elections of December, 1938. The results were a technical victory for the government, but the figures indicated a moral defeat so clearly that the premier resigned. He was replaced by a ministry prepared to take some decisive action about Croat autonomy, which was now a matter of the utmost urgency, for Hitler's seizure of Czechoslovakia in March, 1939 roused such dismay and fury among the Yugoslav fellow-Croats that the problem could no longer be postponed. A degree of federal independence under a coalition central government now became a reality: a desperately necessary but insufficient step towards domestic harmony in face of the impending war. Unfortunately there were still anarchistic elements in Croatia who wanted total separation, and they rashly looked to Hitler for help with this ambition.

The official attitude towards the German war effort, however, was strictly or even blindly neutral, much to the dismay of Yugoslavia's longer-sighted Balkan allies. Prince Paul was trying to pursue his usual policy of non-commitment, but in this case it was useless to pretend the Nazi menace was not there in the hope that it would ultimately go away of its own accord. By early 1941 no more procrastination was possible, and the Yugoslav government decide, like Mr Pickwick, to shout with the biggest crowd; where they failed was in their estimate of the comparative sizes of the "crowds" involved, for they began to make secret overtures to Berlin despite the nationwide hatred which all Yugoslavs felt for the Nazis. The pact with Germany, formed in defiance of such powerful public opinion, was Prince Paul's last official act. When news of it reached the people, which did not take long,

8

outraged feeling coalesced with rare unanimity and erupted into a coup d'état. The ministers were arrested, Paul and his family exiled, and the young King Peter declared of age six months in advance of his eighteenth birthday.

The new government and the Yugoslavian nation were at one in their detestation of the Nazi regime. They made no secret of their hostility and Hitler needed no further excuse. Less than a week after the coup, Germany attacked. Immediately it became obvious that courage and determination were the country's only defence against the invader. Eleven days later came the inevitable surrender. Yugoslavia, little more than twenty years after its establishment, was ruthlessly parcelled out between the various Axis powers and disappeared once more from the German version of the map.

Yugoslavia was not the tamest or the most submissive of Germany's occupied territories. Even the Croats, who had expected Axis support for an independent Croatia, were highly uncertain collaborators, while the Serbs were implacably hostile almost to a man. The first real focus of national resistance was the German invasion of Russia. The Yugoslav monarchy had, not unnaturally, steadily refused to recognize the Bolshevik state. Indeed, the pre-war Yugoslav government had no use for Communism, in Russia or anywhere else, and had outlawed the party in their own country although it was so small as to offer very little threat, but pan-Slavic sympathies now proved stronger than official policies. For the Communists the sufferings of the Russian people in 1941 neatly aligned racial sentiment with political opportunism, and the right man was waiting to take advantage of the moment.

During World War I a Croatian metalworker named Josip Broz was conscripted into the Austrian army. Taken prisoner of war by the Russians, he had not only absorbed his captors' ideology but had risen to an official position of some importance in Moscow. He did not return to his own country until 1938, when he was assigned the (then) rather thankless task of taking over leadership of the dedicated but powerless handful which comprised the Yugoslav Communist party at that time. Few in number the Communists might be, but the Belgrade government thought them worth persecuting, and their leaders were obliged to adopt *noms de guerre*. Josip Broz chose for himself the name of Tito.

Tito was not just a shrewd and well-trained political leader; he was also the highly effective co-ordinator of Communist Partisan movements which were springing up throughout the country. For the most part disorganized and without unanimity of motivation or action, other resistance groups could not compete with Tito's efficient procedures. At first he attracted followers not simply because his cause was calculated to appeal to national sympathy, its mainifestos carefully toned down to avoid frightening off possible right-wing adherents, but because he was successful. A whole series of lightning raids and saboteur attacks provoked hideous retributions, but at that time the people were in a mood of desperation when sacrifice seemed unimportant and effectual action the only hope. However, the Serbian resistance groups known as Chetniks, who were fiercely loyal to the monarchy and opposed to the Partisans' total disregard for the wholesale slaughter of the civilian population, refused to join forces with Tito. Finding himself under attack from the Germans on one side and the Chetniks on the other, Tito was compelled to give up his positions in Serbia and retreat to the mountainous border country. Nazi reprisals in the area were so appalling that it was some years before Tito could overcome Serbian revulsion against the 9 provokers of these atrocities.

Yugoslavia's resistance during the enemy occupation was the familiar drama of heroism and horrors which was being worked out in many European countries while Nazi power was at its height. Hammered savagely into momentary quiescence in one place, the guerillas reappeared in another. In Yugoslavia, however, the Nazis were not the only enemy; the struggle included not only the Germans and the limited but powerful native collaborators but the Chetniks and the Communists with their internecine battles and mutual distrust which sometimes played straight into Axis hands.

In Montenegro, for instance, the Partisans almost succeeded in driving the Italians out. But once again the Communists could not reach any kind of working arrangement with the nationalist forces, and the Italians, taking advantage of this dissension, soon regained control. In Bosnia the local Chetniks found themselves fighting first against the Croatian collaborators, who were engaged in a peculiarly bestial attempt to exterminate the Serbian element of the population, and then alongside the Axis and the Croats against the Partisans, whom they regarded as an even worse alternative. At first those of the Bosnian peasants who did not belong to the Fascist group tried to keep out of the fighting, but under such conditions non-commitment was impossible. When forced to make a choice, they tended increasingly to gravitate to the Partisans, who gradually gained control of more than half the state.

Towards the end of 1942 Tito was in a position to regroup his military forces and restate his political aims. He now commanded eight divisions, which took the field under the grandiloquent title of the "National Army of Liberation and the Partisan Detachment of Yugoslavia". At the same time he called a meeting of politicians, who convened at Bihac to discuss their achievements and their hopes for the future. The statement issued by this body was a masterpiece of innocuous wording. It assured the Yugoslavs (and anyone else who might be interested) that the movement's goal was to liberate the country and to establish a federal democracy. The Red Revolution, it was implied, could not be further from the meeting's thoughts.

This Partisan stock-taking session also compelled the Allies to reassess their own attitude to Yugoslavia. Until now it had been taken for granted that the country was represented by King Peter and the government in exile, but as time went on this body had grown more and more unrealistic. Not only were its members physically at a distance from the people they purported to rule; they were so out of touch with national feeling that they still refused even to admit the existence of the Communist party which was, by now, the only organised political unit in the country apart from the Axis command. Since the Allies had great difficulty in finding out what was really happening inside Yugoslavia, they continued to support the exiled government until a handful of British officers, who infiltrated the country to work with the resistance, realized that to many of the Chetniks the enemy was not the Germans but the Partisans, and that Allied support was bieng used for purely internal political quarrels. Strangely enough, it was the Russians who established the most cordial relations with the royalists government and this, without undermining Tito's belief in the fundamentals of Communism, began to raise doubts among the Yugoslav Partisans about
the desirability of eventual Russian domination.

Despite Russia's failure to provide him with the moral and practical backing he so urgently needed, Tito was in a strong enough position by 1943 to be a real threat to the Nazis, and they decided to launch an all-out offensive against him. Once again the Partisan movement succeeded in fighting off the Axis forces, but came close to destruction at the hands of other Yugoslavs. Driven back by a concerted German and Italian attack, Tito planned a strategic retreat to the cover of the inaccessible Montenegrin mountains, but when he reached the river Neretva he found his way barred by twelve thousand Chetnik troops and it was only after a fierce struggle that he broke through to temporary safety. Even in the mountains, however, the Partisans were not left in peace.

The Axis decided, now that the resistance forces were on the defensive, that it was time to wipe them out once and for all. The Germans were efficient soldiers and never too hide-bound to learn from enemy tactics when these seemed appropriate and successful. They accordingly began to use the Partisans' own methods of shock attacks by small mobile units rather than pitched battles against an elusive enemy. The Germans had plentiful supplies of infinitely superior munitions, and Tito's men had to fight their way through two months which they afterwards remembered as the most desperate of the entire war before they reached breathing space in north-eastern Bosnia. Their losses were terrible, but their spirit of defiance was completely undaunted. When their next chance came six months later it found them recovered and ready.

This opportunity, which brought a dramatic change to Tito's fortunes, was the surrender of Italy, which took place in September, 1943, leaving a large part of Slovenia, Dalmatia and Montenegro unoccupied. The Germans moved quickly to seize the former Italian-held provinces, but Tito was faster and won not only a good deal of territory but — even more important — a large quantity of invaluable equipment and weapons. The Partisans were not able to hold on to the land for long in face of a determined German onslaught, but their gains were still considerable, not only in terms of the munitions they acquired but of improved morale within Yugoslavia and increased prestige for their movement among the Allies.

Germany's enemies at large were now compelled to see the exiled government for what it was: an out-of-touch obsolete survival without any real meaning or power in its own country. Furthermore, a certain amount of reliable information was now filtering out of the Balkans, and the Allies received confirmation of their earlier suspicions that the help they had supplied to the Chetnik resistance groups was being used not against the Axis but to further the royalist political cause, sometimes even in active collaboration with the Germans, against the Partisans who were the only truly effective anti-Nazi force in Yugoslavia. At the beginning of 1944 Winston Churchill announced in the House of Commons that no further aid would be sent to the Chetniks and that in future all Allied support would go to Tito, now Marshal of Yugoslavia and premier of the National Liberation government. At this point King Peter, who seems to have taken a more realistic view of the situation than his *ci-devant* ministers, broadcast a statement proclaiming his recognition of Marshal Tito's powers and his own intention of remaining in exile until the will of the people could be ascertained by a referendum.

All these speculations about Yugoslavia's future political constitution were a trifle premature in 1944, for the country was still held in an iron grip by the Nazis. As late as May, 1944 an air attack on the Marshal's headquarters forced him to escape as best he could and make a run for Italy, now in Allied hands. However, he made good use of this enforced retreat to confer with the commanders of the Allied Mediterranean troops and Mr Churchill about Yugoslavia's contribution to the already foreseeable process of finishing off Germany and bringing the war to an end.

At least Tito was unlikely to meet with much hostility from his own people by this stage. Even in Serbia the Chetniks had lost most of their supporters, partly because of their occasional acts of collaboration, partly because of the withdrawal of Allied aid, and partly because it was obvious by now that they were on the losing side. The Russian army was advancing into the Balkans and Tito's troops began to push forward to join up with them, while the Marshal himself made a provident journey to Moscow to secure a promise that any Yugoslav territory liberated by the Reds would be returned to Yugoslav administration as soon as hostilities ended. Meanwhile the Russians and the Partisans drove the Germans out of Belgrade and in the process the remnants of the Serbian Chetniks were swept away. A few months more of hard fighting were still to come in Serbia and the northern provinces, but these, though they caused desperate men to commit some of the most revolting atrocities of the war, were in the nature of a mopping-up operation; Tito was already beginning to switch his personal role from soldier to statesman as he tackled the question of Yugoslavia's future.

So far his relations with Britain and America had been as cordial as they are ever likely to be between people upholding such different ideologies, but all this goodwill came to a sad and abrupt end over the city of Trieste. Tito wanted the city for Yugoslavia, and his troops had fought for it until the very day of the German surrender. The Allies, however, insisted on returning Trieste to Italy, and with a good deal of bitterness Tito was forced to concur. He hoped that the Russians would support his claim, but they had no wish to risk a major confrontation with the other Allies or to alienate the powerful and numerous Italian Communist party, and once again they let him down.

The niceties of diplomatic sparring on an international level were a luxury which would have to wait, for conditions inside Yugoslavia were indescribably chaotic. After so many years of merciless warfare a large proportion of the labour force were dead, all services were disrupted, the currency was debased, there were places where one stone standing on another could hardly be found, and every amenity with the slightest strategic value had been destroyed. Since these strategic amenities included bridges, roads, railways, airports, factories and practically everything else that Yugoslavia had built up so laboriously in its struggle towards industrialization between the wars, the problems of starting again were little short of gargantuan. One of the few advantages Tito could count on was a virtually free hand. The only organized power in the land was the Partisan army, still functioning and in charge of all civil administration (such as it was) in default of any viable alternative. Officially a provisional government including representatives of all political parties had assembled in Belgrade immediately after the capital's liberation, but since the army was running the country and Tito was running the army, nobody was in any kind of position to challenge his decrees.

His first moves were made with a view to stabilizing and strengthening the Communist regime so as to put it on an acceptable democratic footing. Coinage reform, which divided the value of existing money by ten, and a sweeping nationalization programme virtually wiped out the petit bourgeoisie at one stroke and reduced most of the population to an equality of dependence on the state. The few remaining non-Communist politicians could see clearly enough which way things were going, but they could do nothing to stop it; their combined numbers in the provisional assembly only amounted to eight against the Communists' twenty, and they had no leader with anything like the popular prestige and personal glamour of Tito, the legendary hero who had driven out the Germans and who promised to provide fair shares for everybody after so many years of bitter hardship. Before the elections the assembly made provision for parliament with two houses: the Federal Council with 319 members, and the Council of Nationalities to represent the separate interests of the various provinces. Then, with little optimism on the part of anyone but the Communists, they went to the polls. Since the only candidates were those of the People's Front, who supported the official Communist programme, the results were a foregone conclusion. The only unusual thing about the voting was that hardly any of the dragooned electorate was unhappy about it.

The new government, with the enthusiastic support of the people and the able leadership of Marshal Tito, convened in November, 1945 to see about the reconstruction of their shattered country. They began, inevitably, by abolishing the monarchy and proclaiming the Federal People's Republic of Yugoslavia, with a constitution based on that of the Soviet Union as settled in 1936. That was the easy part. Putting these principles into practice was a good deal more complicated.

In any predominantly agricultural country the first and most vital step towards socialism is land reform. In Yugoslavia much of the land was held by private owners and a large part of it was covered with forests. These were sequestrated by the government and the big estates were redistributed according to a ruling that no individual might hold more than thirty-five hectares (87½ acres). A number of peasants who had previously been landless tenants working chiefly for the benefit of others now found themselves owners of the land they worked, while others from barren regions were resettled in more fertile areas. Needless to say, these measures were extremely popular among people who were able to be independent and self-supporting for the first time in their lives, but the peasants regarded the state's attempts to initiate collective farming, with fixed prices for produce and high taxation on profits, as totally incompatible with their traditional way of life.

As befits a good democracy, full religious toleration for all creeds became statutory. The only stipulation was that no sect might interfere in politics or urge actions or beliefs frowned on by the state. Unfortunately, formally structured religions such as Roman Catholicism or Orthodoxy (to which at least three-quarters of the population subscribed) do not mix happily with Communism, and it was not long before the penalty clauses in the toleration decree came into operation. It is to the government's credit that churches were untouched and priests fulminated from the pulpit with relative impunity, but newspapers were wound up, schools closed and colleges disbanded. The Orthodox and Moslem faiths accepted these restrictions philosophically and continued to operate within the limits prescribed by the

13

state, but the Roman Catholics could not settle for secular domination; their first obedience was owed to the Vatican and nobody but the Pope himself could absolve them from this requirement. In the end the government broke off diplomatic relations with the Vatican, but the churches were still permitted to function although the state grants for paying priests and maintaining buildings enjoyed by the Moslem and Orthodox believers were withdrawn from the Catholics.

Once the blueprint for the future had been drawn up, money was needed for the rebuilding programme. The United Nations provided the initial $425 million, which were used to re-establish industry, communications and agriculture, but much more was wanted to carry Yugoslavia over the first five-year period. Tito hoped that the people of the Soviet Union would come to the rescue of their brother Communists, and to begin with, cash, technicians and favourable trade terms were generously made available; but before the five-year plan was completed, the honeymoon with the Kremlin was already over and divorce was well on the way. In June 1948 the six Communist groups whose alliance is known as the Cominform announced to a startled world that henceforth Yugoslavia was no longer to be counted among their ranks. There had been no previous intimations of this break, and the reasons for it, as proclaimed by the Soviet Union, were purely ideological: the Yugoslavs simply were not good Marxists, and refused to reform even when the error of their ways was pointed out to them. Furthermore, they would not rebel against the author of these enormities when invited to do so, and such wilful perversity could not be tolerated. There was, of course, more to it than that. The real reason for Yugoslavia's expulsion from the Cominform was that Tito and his government sturdily persisted in doing what they believed was best for their country instead of sedulously toeing the Kremlin party line.

Tito's defiant independence was all very admirable, but it left his country in an extremely difficult position. Economic help, technical instruction and the majority of Yugoslavia's imports and exports all depended on the goodwill of the Soviet Union, which was now withdrawn. However, if the West expected Tito to react to the situation by selling out to capitalism, they were as mistaken as Moscow had been; he continued to pursue his own policies and after Stalin's death it was Russia, not Yugoslavia, which made the first tentative moves towards reconciliation, which has never been fully effected.

The years immediately after the break with the Cominform were hard for Yugoslavia. Debts rose and production fell as a drought in 1950 added poor harvests to the numerous other problems facing the people. There was necessarily some easing of the tension which had affected Yugoslav relations with the West, as Britain and the USA were now supplying some of the aid which had previously come from Russia, but Tito was not prepared to modify his own interpretation of Communism for the sake of an economic hand-out. Gradually, by the sheer hard work, determination and courage of the people, Yugoslavia's policy of non-commitment began to pay off. Where they had no cranes or bulldozers they used baskets and wheelbarrows to build essential modern installations. Industrialization increased at an amazing rate and agricultural production rose again after 1953 when co-operative farming came to an end, killed off by the silent but stubborn opposition of the peasantry. The government, always pragmatic, allowed it to die without comment.

14   While the smothering folds of the Iron Curtain were enveloping eastern Europe, Tito's

Yugoslavia still kept an opening towards the West, and no Cominform pressure has been able to make him close it. The people are passionately convinced that Communism is right for them, but it is strictly their own home-made brand of Communism, and as time goes on it has become quietly but steadily more liberal. There are fewer secret police and political prisoners, tourists are encouraged, much to the benefit of international understanding, and there is a free exchange of scientific knowledge and literature. The arts are no longer confined to the stultifying canons of "socialist realism" and the standard of living of the ordinary people has improved beyond recognition with the increase of national prosperity. There are still plenty of problems to be solved, such as the persistent distrust and hostility which survives between some regional groups, but the Yugoslavs' hopes for the future are justifiably high.

Anne G. Ward

The visitor who enters Yugoslavia by the main motorway from Munich to Ljubljana immediately encounters the lovely mountain region of the Julian Alps. The beauty of the scenery and the high but sheltered slopes make this an ideal location for winter sports, which can be continued for six months out of every year. Between the mountains is a delightful valley in which lies a tiny village named Trenta, a short distance from Soca along the banks of the river Soca. The region depends for a livelihood almost exclusively on its natural beauty, which attracts large numbers of visitors all year round.

16

One of the most beautiful and popular tourist centres in Slovenia is Bled. It stands on the shores of Lake Bled, in the centre of which is a small island bearing a steepled church dedicated to the Virgin Mary. The lake itself is not without interest. It is glacial in origin and very deep (some 155 feet), but in spite of this, and of the fact that it is usually frozen over in winter, the water in summer becomes unusually warm, sometimes reaching a temperature of 75 deg F. This is attributed to the presence of warm mineral springs with a high iron content in the bed of the lake, the water from which has helped to give Bled its character as a health resort.

Ljubljana, the capital of Slovenia, is a fascinating mixture of ancient and modern. Local legends claim that it was founded by Jason and the Argonauts, and there are definite records of a Roman city there in the First Century AD. Its chequered history has included invasions and occupations by the Huns, the Franks, the Venetians and Turks, the armies of Napoleon, who made it the capital of .Illyria, and the Hapsburgs, who controlled it until the end of World War 1. It is now one of the most important meeting-points for the connections between the Balkans and central Europe, and since 1945 has attained a high standard of prosperity and dignity, with many fine new buildings alongside the picturesque survivals of the old town.

20

One of the oldest and most picturesque towns in Slovenia is Ptuj, which lies in a beautiful location on the river Drava between Maribor and Varazdin. The town was first settled by the Celts in the pre-Christian era, and a Roman camp was established there by the emperor Octavian. After years of harassment by the Huns, Goths and Turks, it was fortified by the Slovenes. The Baroque castle with triple-arcaded inner courtyard in the town centre has now been converted into a museum, which houses not only local Roman and Slavic antiquities but a fine art

collection.

The visitor to the town of Maribor should begin by deciding whether he prefers modern progress or ancient charm, as both amenities are fully represented, one on each side of the river Drava. On the right bank are the workshops and factories of the modern town, which is an important industrial centre, while the historic city lies on the left bank. The Sixteenth Century town hall flanks an attractive old market place, and near the river bank is the *Burg*. Built in the Fourteenth Century, it was the local centre of judicial administration, and still preserves a remarkably fine contemporary staircase and painted ceiling.

The road from Ljubljana to Zagreb mainly
follows the course of the river Sava.
Branching off this river is a tributary called
the Krka, which flows through a pleasant
valley in which lies the small town of Novo
Mesto. The water-course provides excellent
fishing and is associated with the popular
mineral springs at nearby Dolenjske Toplice.
In the fertile valley an occasional fall
furnishes power for the little water mills
which support the local cottage industries.

Zuzemberk castle, a hereditary seat of the counts of Auersparg, stands in the middle of a small town on the river Krka. Mentioned as early as 1293, it was extensively altered and restored in the early decades of the Eighteenth Century. It has massive towers at each corner and the walls were once surmounted by battlements. During the fighting in World War II the castle was reduced to ruins, and the damage was so far-reaching that repairs have not proved feasible. Zuzemberk is reached by following the course of the river Krka from Novo Mosto.

Polhov Gradec is a tiny village in Slovenia, so small that it seldom appears on maps. The whole village centres on the castle and its park, in which stands the early Baroque Neptune Fountain. This is a square cistern with a short column at each corner, on which stand statues representing different aspects of rural life. In the centre of the cistern, a taller column supports a figure of the god Neptune. The castle of Polhov Gradec was destroyed in World War II, but has since been restored and now serves as a modern tourist centre.

St Stephen's Cathedral, which stands next to the Seventeenth-Century archbishop's palace in Zagreb, originally dated back to the Thirteenth Century, but after extensive repairs it was entirely rebuilt in the pseudo-Gothic style during the Nineteenth Century. All the most ancient works of art from the cathedral were removed for safe keeping at this time. Zagreb is the capital of Croatia and its central position ·gives it considerable strategic and commercial importance. It lies on the ground between the foothills of Mount Zagreb and the river Sava. The oldest part is the High Town, which was once enclosed in the fortification wall built at the same time as St Stephen's Cathedral.

In the Low Town of Zagreb, just south of St Stephen's Cathedral, lies the modern market *(Dolac)* which, like the Rialto in Venice, still occupies the site of the city's most ancient commercial centre. The stall-holders, who bring their wares in from the surrounding countryside, often wear the colourful Yugoslavian national dress. The streets around the market are among the oldest and most architecturally distinguished in Zagreb. At No 10 Opaticka Street, near the archbishop's palace and library, stands the Paravic mansion with its fine wrought iron gates and a fountain in the forecourt.

Cyril and Methodius Street in the High Town of Zagreb leads to the Thirteenth-Century Gothic church of St Mark in Stjepan Radic Square. An unusual feature of this striking building is the roof, which is carried out in brilliantly coloured tiles incorporating the coats of arms of Dalmatia, Croatia, Slavonia and the city of Zagreb. The church is surrounded by a number of Eighteenth Century and Nineteenth Century mansions which now serve as judicial and municipal offices, while the east side of the square is occupied by the Parliament building.

36

The town of Varazdin in north-eastern Croatia is now a rapidly expanding industrial centre with a flourishing textile business. Its importance, which arises partly from its position on the banks of the river Drava, dates back to the Middle Ages, when it enjoyed the enviable status of a Free City. The fortifications from this period, which are unusually well preserved, lie among the gardens and waterside walks with which the town is richly provided, offering a pleasant visual contrast to the surrounding evidence of modern prosperity.

One of the most pleasant resorts on the
Adriatic coast is the town of Piran. occupied
by the Venetians in 1283 and under their
control for many years, it preserves a
number of architectural features strongly
reminiscent of typical Venetian building
styles, with beautiful loggias and arcades.
On the hill behind the city stands the
imposing Baroque structure of the church of
St George with its adjoining campanile, built
in 1607 on the model of that of the Piazza
San Marco in Venice. The hexagonal
Baptistery next to the campanile dates to the
same period and its font is made from a
Second Century Roman sarcophagus.

Pula is·the largest and most important town n Istria, and the centre of the regional administration. This pre-eminence is no recent phenomenon, for the town is richly endowed with Roman remains, some of which are in an excellent state of preservation. Perhaps the most impressive is the amphitheatre, locally known as the arena, which is the sixth largest surviving structure of this type. Built by Augustus (Octavian) early in the first century AD, it was enlarged by Claudius and Vespasian. It was barely saved from being dismantled and removed bodily· to Venice by the protests of a public-spirited Venetian senator named Gabriele Emo, whose altruism is recorded on a plaque set in the wall of the west tower.

42

The peninsular town of Rovinj, like many other Adriatic coast resorts, owes many of its most attractive architectural features to Venice, but the natural beauty of its setting is unique and has lured a populous artists' colony to the district. In the middle of the headland is a green hill which has wisely been preserved with little or no building to spoil its freshness and to distract attention from the town's finest monument. Crowning this eminence and dominating the town is the Baroque church of St Euphemia, built in 1736, which contains the original Sixth Century sarcophagus of the saint. A campanile designed in 1677 by Manopole in the Venetian style adjoins the church.

44

The main square of Rovinj is named, like so many modern Yugoslav complexes, after Marshal Tito. It opens on the harbour, where pleasure craft lie moored alongside local fishing boats. Venetian influence is once more clearly to be seen in the clock tower, with its double-arched entry, so strongly reminiscent of the Torre dell' Orologio in Venice. Just behind this square lies the oldest part of the town, with its numerous Venetian houses. Rovinj has so many connections with the city across the Adriatic that it has become the centre for Italian studies in Istria.

46

Rijeka's location at the mouth of the river Rjecina, together with its sheltered natural harbour and its easy communication with most of the northern inland cities, have made it a prosperous centre for many centuries. Commerce, culture and industry all flourish there, and the dock area is usually equally crowded with sightseers and workers. The town has a long history of chequered fortunes, as it passed from Austrian to Hungarian domination and came under attack by the Venetians, who saw its prosperity as a threat to their own commercial supremacy. It then achieved independence, fell to Napoleon, reverted to the Austro-Hungarian empire, and finally achieved unity and assimilation with Yugoslavia in 1924.

The Plitvice lakes *(Plitvicka jezera)* are a continuous chain of lakes and waterfalls situated about ninety miles inland from Senj. They lie in a national park of great beauty where all the natural life and landscape features are very strictly protected, and it is pleasant to know that this far-sighted concern for environmental factors will preserve the lakes in their present unspoilt condition. Roads and footpaths along the waterside give fine views over the four miles of lakes and falls, several of which are more than 200 feet high. The larger lakes are used as boating centres.

The village of Karlobag on the Adriatic coast
lies at the mouth of the Velebitski Canal. The
centre of the village was once a huge
Fourteenth Century castle round which the
rest of the settlement grew up. Sacked by
the Turks, it was rebuilt in 1579 and its
remains still crown the hill near the town.
The Austrians hoped to promote Karlobag as
a port to act as an outlet for the region
immediately inland, but its chief importance
today lies in its function as a terminal for the
ferry boat service connecting the mainland
with Pag, a large island a short distance out
52 in the Adriatic.

Zadar is the biggest and one of the most important towns on the north Dalmatian coast. Its history dates back to at least the Ninth Century BC, and Greeks, Romans, Byzantines and Venetians have all left traces of their passing there. The extensive Roman Forum, with its broken classical columns, contains many more recent buildings, including the curious circular church of St Donatus. Its design is so original that there is some difficulty in dating this unique building, with its Roman floor and unusual drum-shaped interior nearly 90 feet high, but it is believed to belong to the reign of the Byzantine emperor Porphyrogenitus, who mentions it in AD 949.

Tito Quay runs along the seaward shore of
Trogir, a compact little island town linked to
the mainland a few miles north of Split by a
causeway. Trogir preserves an unusual
number of Gothic and medieval buildings
which, though once badly neglected, now
give the town an attractively picturesque
atmosphere. Conspicuous in the middle of
the tree-lined esplanade is the Fourteenth
Century Dominican church with its
campanile, and in the foreground is a corner
of the Kamerlengo fortress, a large Venetian
castle with towers and battlements, built in
1424-37 to command the approach to the
harbour — a highly necessary precaution in
those days, when piracy was rife.

56

The cathedral of St Lawrence in Trogir was begun in the Romanesque period, razed by the Saracens, and not finally completed until 1250. The west door, largely concealed by a Romanesque arch, is one of the finest existing examples of the Gothic-Romanesque style. Completed in 1240 by an otherwise unkown local master named Radovan, it is richly carved with saints, animals, symbolic figures and calender scenes showing rural life appropriate to each month of the year. The lunette above the door shows several scenes from the Nativity, with flying angels and cherubs in attendance.

The whole of the Old Town *(Stari Grad)* of Split is contained in the enclosure of the Roman walls of Diocletian's palace. This able and determined emperor, who ruled from AD 284 to 305, gave the empire a last lease of life before its final dissolution, but his greatest wish was always to retire to his home on the Dalmatian coast. Few men can have realized their ambition so satisfactorily, for the palace he built is still in an excellent state of preservation, and dictates the layout of the surrounding streets to a great extent. Tito Quay, which runs along the waterfront of the port, is flanked on the inland side by the facade of the palace, much of which is still

occupied.

The main waterside entrance to Diocletian's palace at Split is the Porta Argentea (Silver Gate). It was badly damaged during World War II, but intelligent and discriminating repairs have gone a long way to restoring it to its former dignity. It is, in fact, better displayed now than it has been at any time since the Seventeenth Century, when it was hidden by some fortifications and a church built by the Venetians. On either side of the gate are the ruins of octagonal towers, which once defended the entrance to the palace against attack by water. The addition of the promenade protects the frontage of the palace from damage by the sea which formerly washed up against its walls.

The charming medieval city of Korcula lies on a small peninsula at the eastern end of the island of the same name, within easy sight of the Dalmatian coast. The streets were scientifically planned so as to use the rising ground to catch the morning and evening sun while avoiding the fiercest of the midday heat. It is one of the few functional towns where the majority of the buildings are well preserved Gothic and Renaissance in style, and is still largely surrounded by its Fourteenth Century wall. The huge Balbi Tower in the foreground flanks the yacht basin, and behind it stands the Lombard Tower which defended the governor's palace. The cathedral in the background, with its attractive lanterned bell-tower, was chiefly built in the Fifteenth Century.

The small town of Jajce occupies a delightful situation on the banks of the river Vrbas, surrounded by richly wooded mountains on either side. For a short time in the Fifteenth Century it was the capital of Bosnia, and the tombs of the Bosnian Kings are still preserved there, but today its importance is chiefly industrial. Just to the west of Jajce the river Pliva, a tributary of the Vrbas, plunges over a series of spectacularly beautiful cataracts, some of which are harnessed to power ancient water mills.

66

A few miles inland from the swampy delta of the river Neretva lies the village of Pocitelj, clinging to the rising ground above the modern motor road. This is one of the many places in Yugoslavia which betray evidence of Turkish occupation. Pocitelj is, in fact, a well-preserved example of a Turkish walled town, and has a fine mosque dating to 1563. In the neighbourhood of Pocitelj, which lies just inside the Bosnia-Hercegovina border, is an ancient necropolis containing the ornamented tombs of the Bogomil sect.

The town of Mostar, which straddles the Neretva river in a beautiful mountain gorge, occupies such a sheltered site that it is famous for the mildness of its climate. This is similar to that of the Mediterranean shores, and produces several varieties of subtropical flowers and trees, which are not generally found in this part of Yugoslavia. The bridge, built by the Turks in the Sixteenth Century, is a particularly elegant span guarded at each end by a tower. The modern town on the right bank is a flourishing industrial centre, but the old city on the left still preserves its narrow winding mediaeval streets and a number of mosques and minarets.

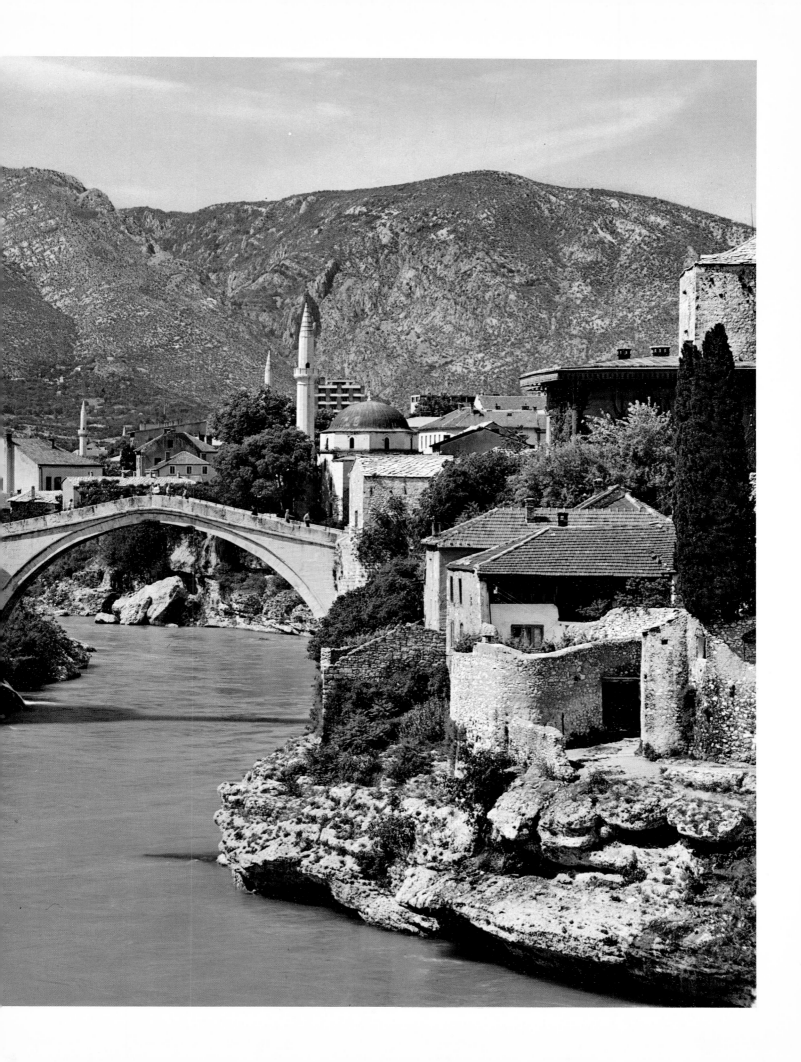

Dubrovnik, like so many Yugoslavian towns on the Adriatic coast, is built on a small peninsula. The old town, which contains most of the interesting antiquities within the surviving circuit of its walls, lies at the foot of Mount Srdj, with modern suburbs on either side. The old town is one of the best preserved and attractive mediaeval centres in Europe, and the fact that no motor traffic is permitted in its streets adds to its notable charm. Once the independent republic of Ragusa, the town fell upon hard times in the Eighteenth and Nineteenth Centuries, but this had at least the merit of preserving it from the current mania for indiscriminate and ill-formed reonstruction which has done so much damage in many places.

72

There are only two major European cities where the pedestrian can walk in peace, safe from the harassment of the internal combustion engine. One is Venice, and the other is the old city of Dubrovnik, where a highly intelligent city ordinance has banished motor transport to the modern suburbs. The Prid Dvorom in the heart of the old city is flanked on one side by the church of St Blaise, which is distinguished by its unusual north/south orientation, and on the other by a harmonious row of buildings above a handsome arcade. At the end of the Prid Dvorom is the Palaca Sponza, a pleasant blending of Gothic and Renaissance styles with a fine colonnaded loggia.

Perast is an unusual little township. Its time of prosperity was short, and as a result almost all the buildings belong to the Baroque period, which gives the town a remarkable appearance of architectural unity. Few are outstanding, but all have a pleasant quiet elegance. The town is laid out along the sea front, which is lined with palm trees, and the houses which formerly belonged to ship-owners and captains flank the promenade. Five minutes' boat ride from the shore are two small islands, the treeless one of which is a man-made structure based on an underwater reef. It is reinforced every year during a festival in which decorated boats bring fresh stones to deposit round the shore.

76

The gulf of Kotor is one of the finest stretches of natural scenery on the whole of the Adriatic coast. It is hemmed in on either side by high barren mountains like those of a Norwegian fjord, but lower down by the waterside the vegetation is brilliantly colourful and luxurious. The abrupt rise and fall of the ground make the gulf subject to violent changes of weather, with heavy rainfall and frequent thunderstorms. The gulf is so spectacular that steamers make excursions from the neighbouring resorts and even as far afield as Dubrovnik to enable visitors to admire the views.

The ancient city of Budva on the Montenegrin coast is also a highly popular modern holiday resort. The old city is encircled by a wall which was built in the Fifteenth Century during the Venetian occupation, destroyed by an earthquake in 1667 and repaired in an attempt to keep out the Turkish invaders. The view from the citadel over the picturesque roofs of the old town takes in the curve of the bay, where the sheltered sandy beaches are attracting an increasing number of tourists, whose arrival has, perhaps unfortunately for the architectural atmosphere, been accompanied by the usual outbreak of modern hotels and amusement centres.

The Fourteenth Century rulers of Serbia were powerful and prosperous and evidence of their wealth still survives in the great monastery of Decani, which they endowed near Pec. Built by Stevan III Decanski and his son Dusan in 1335, the monastery is now in a ruinous condition, but the church is a well-preserved example of the local blending of Romanesque, Gothic and Byzantine architectural styles. Unlike most contemporary religious buildings, it is not cruciform, but is designed as a basilica surmounted by a cupola. Each of the arcades which surround the roof and the cupola has a fantastically carved animal head for a finial.

82

The sea at Budva washes directly against the walls and buildings which form the waterfront fortifications of the peninsula. The town's need for strong defences was great in its early days. Founded (or so legend has it) by Cadmus, King of Phoenicia, it has been successively occupied by Greeks, Illyrians, Romans, Byzantines, Saracens and Serbians. It achieved independence and self-government briefly in the Fourteenth Century, but barely a hundred years later it was absorbed into the Venetian empire. After the fall of Venice, Budva remained chiefly under Austrian domination until the formation of the modern Yugoslav state.

84

The tiny village of Rasanac, near Petrovac, houses an entirely agricultural community. The mountain country behind the coast is harsh, and some of the fields have been painfully and laboriously formed by hand, the peasants carrying the earth from the valleys to any suitable hollow in the rocks. Nearer the coast, however, the land has a truly Mediterranean richness, with olive groves running almost to the water's edge. The farms are prosperous, and the people who live in this favoured region seldom encounter the hardships faced by their mountain neighbours.

The tiny island village of Sveti Stefan has been entirely converted into one of the most original and charming hotel colonies in the world. Joined to the mainland by a causeway running along the top of a sand bar, it boasts all the most modern amenities, but they are ingeniously disguised in the Fifteenth and Sixteenth Century buildings which are in themselves a focal point of attraction for tourists. Originally founded by the Pastrovici, it was an autonomous settlement under the Venetian empire and in the Sixteenth Century stout fortifications were added to keep the Turks at bay.

88

The road from Kotor to Cetinje must be one of the most picturesque in Yugoslavia. It climbs up the hills behind the bay of Kotor, passing the remains of the old Venetian fortifications, and then makes for the foothills of Lovcen, on a track cut through sheer rock for much of the way. As it winds and twists through the mountains, a fresh and beautiful view meets the eye at every turn. The landscape is craggy and apparently deserted, as the region is too barren to support more than a very few peasant farms, which eke out a precarious existence wherever a fold in the hills provides a pocket of earth.

90

The resort of Petrovac owes its prosperity very largely to its beautiful surroundings in a bay sheltered by the mountains. Now a popular holiday centre with a fine promenade and modern hotels, there is also an old town built in the local style, with steeply pitched roofs as a protection against the winter winds. Vines, fig trees and olives grow profusely in the district, and the sand of the beach is believed to have medicinal properties. Petrovac even boasts a marine grotto which can only be entered by water, and is renowned for the unearthly lighting effects it produces.

92

Prizren, which lies in the valley below Mount Sar, is a picturesque town built very much in the oriental style. This is scarcely surprising, since the town was in Turkish hands from 1454 until 1912. Like many cities which were formerly part of the Turkish dominions, Prizren has acquired a considerable reputation for the production of fine metalwork. The focal point of the town is the great mosque of Sinan Pasha, which was almost entirely constructed in 1615 from building materials pillaged by the Turks from the monastery of St Archangel.

94

Prizren, on the river Bistrica, was once a town of considerable importance carrying on a flourishing trade with Dubrovnik and exercising great influence on the surrounding districts. Tsar Dusan the Great made it his capital in the Fourteenth Century, when it even had its own mint. It subsequently came under Turkish control, and the Turks converted the great church to Islamic worship and added a mosque. It is now chiefly known for skilled craftsmanship in metalworking, embroidery and silk.

96

On the shore of lake Ohrid stands the town of the same name, one of the oldest in Macedonia. The whole of the surrounding region along the shore of the lake is dotted with ancient and venerable religious foundations. Many of these buildings are finely-preserved specimens of the purest style of Byzantine architecture, and some of them contain wall paintings dating back to the eleventh century and earlier. The church of Svet Jovan stands on the shore of lake Ohrid, which is geologically one of the oldest in the world. It is of outstanding interest to zoologists as it contains shellfish of a type which belongs to the Tertiary Age, and are the only known survivals of this era.

The town of Prilep at the foot of Mount Babuna lies on one of the main road leading to the Yugoslav-Greek border. It is now a centre of the tobacco industry, but it has ancient associations with the legendary hero Kraljevic Marko. A small road runs from the city in a due westerly direction past the ruins of the Fourteenth Century city of Marko, and after passing through some spectacularly beautiful mountain scenery, it reaches the holiday resort town of Krusevo, seen here. Now almost exclusively devoted to recreation, it was once the site of the Macedonian rising against the Turks.

100

Skopje is the capital and chief city of Yugoslavian Macedonia. It occupies a commanding position on the main road to Thessalonike and on the river Vardar, which runs through the middle of the town dividing it into the old and the new cities, the latter dating only to the Nineteenth Century. One of the most impressive monuments of the old town is the Fifteenth Century mosque of Mustapha Pasha with its graceful minaret, which stands in its own gardens with a magnificent view over the town and the surrounding mountains. Built in 1470 by the great Turkish commander of that name, it is still in use for Islamic worship today.

The village of Bujanovac lies on the road from Nis to Skopje, a few miles south of Vranje, just inside the Serbian border. Life is not easy for the villagers and peasants of the region. There is little of historic or artistic interest around Bujanovac to attract the ubiquitous tourist who supplements the economy of more favoured districts, but despite their many privations the inhabitants preserve an air of cheerful sociability which lightens the atmosphere of their village. The small houses are whitewashed or painted in colours which, unlike those used in the majority of folk arts, are sometimes remarkably subtle and sophisticated.

104

Belgrade, capital of Serbia and of the Federative Republic of Yugoslavia, lies on the right bank of the Danube at its junction with the Sava. The city suffered severely in both world wars, but particularly the second, during which whole districts were wiped out and the antiquities of the old fortress were badly damaged, but since 1945 an energetic and enlightened rebuilding programme has raised the new city to an eminence worthy of its position as an influential European capital. One of the broadest and most handsome streets in Belgrade is the Avenue of the National Revolution, on which stands the modern Parliament building, opposite the Praesidium of the National Council.

The monastery church of Gracanica a few miles south of Pristina is one of the finest surviving examples of medieval Serbian architecture. Built in 1321 by Milutin Nemanjic, king of Serbia, it became the seat of the bishops of Ljipljan. In the early fifteen-hundreds it already had a printing press and was turning out religious texts. The church is built in the form of a double cross with cupolas at the intersection, the simple undecorated brickwork and dressed stone of the exterior enhancing the complex harmony of the design. The church has been pillaged more than once in its long history, but the fine Fourteenth Century frescoes of the interior remain undamaged.

Makarska is the only town of any size on the Dalmatian coast between Split and Dubrovnik. Most of the town's buildings of the Baroque period were destroyed during the bombardments of World War II and it is now predominantly a modern resort. Its setting, however, is remarkably beautiful. It lies at the foot of the Biokovo mountain range, the highest on the Dalmatian coast, on a sheltered bay with sandy beaches stretching for more than two miles. Backed by pine woods running down close to the water's edge, Makarska offers spectacularly lovely views of the sunset over the Adriatic and the offshore islands.